# MAN-MADE DISASTERS
# CHALLENGER

## by Jenny Fretland VanVoorst

pogo

# Ideas for Parents and Teachers

Pogo Books let children practice reading informational text while introducing them to nonfiction features such as headings, labels, sidebars, maps, and diagrams, as well as a table of contents, glossary, and index.

Carefully leveled text with a strong photo match offers early fluent readers the support they need to succeed.

## Before Reading

- "Walk" through the book and point out the various nonfiction features. Ask the student what purpose each feature serves.

- Look at the glossary together. Read and discuss the words.

## Read the Book

- Have the child read the book independently.

- Invite him or her to list questions that arise from reading.

## After Reading

- Discuss the child's questions. Talk about how he or she might find answers to those questions.

- Prompt the child to think more. Ask: Did you know about the *Challenger* explosion before reading this book? What more do you want to learn after reading it?

Pogo Books are published by Jump!
5357 Penn Avenue South
Minneapolis, MN 55419
www.jumplibrary.com

Library of Congress Cataloging-in-Publication Data

Names: Fretland VanVoorst, Jenny, 1972- author.
Title: Challenger / by Jenny Fretland VanVoorst.
Description: Minneapolis, MN: Jump!, Inc., [2018]
Series: Man-made disasters | Audience: Ages 7-10.
Includes bibliographical references and index.
Identifiers: LCCN 2017038110 (print)
LCCN 2017037433 (ebook)
ISBN 9781624967016 (ebook)
ISBN 9781620319147 (hardcover: alk. paper)
ISBN 9781620319154 (pbk.)
Subjects: LCSH: Challenger (Spacecraft)—Accidents—Juvenile literature. | Space vehicle accidents—United States—Juvenile literature.
Classification: LCC TL867 (print) | LCC TL867 .F74 2018 (ebook) | DDC 363.12/465/0973—dc23
LC record available at https://lccn.loc.gov/2017038110

Editor: Kristine Spanier
Book Designer: Michelle Sonnek
Photo Researcher: Michelle Sonnek

Photo Credits: JSC/NASA, cover, 1 (astronauts), 9, 14-15, 20-21 (shuttle); Gillmar/Shutterstock, 1 (frame); Mega Pixel/Shutterstock, 1 (shuttle); urbanbuzz/Shutterstock, 3; trekandshoot/Shutterstock, 4 (tv); vectorfusionart/Shutterstock, 4 (reporter); Bettman/Getty, 4 (shuttle), 10-11; NASA, 5, 8, 20-21 (logo); Bruce Weaver/AP Photo, 6-7; Everett Historical/Shutterstock, 12-13, 18-19; wavebreakmedia/Shutterstock, 16 (woman); Syracuse Newspapers/The Image Works, 16 (newspaper); NC Collections/Alamy, 17; Stocktrek Images, Inc./Alamy, 20-21 (satellite); DwaFotografy/Shutterstock, 20-21 (tablet); Annmarie Young/Shutterstock, 23 (right); Rocky89/iStock, 23 (left).

Printed in the United States of America at Corporate Graphics in North Mankato, Minnesota.

# TABLE OF CONTENTS

# CHAPTER 1

# A COLD DAY TO LAUNCH

It was January 28, 1986. **NASA** had been sending shuttles into space for five years. But today was special. *Challenger* was set to launch. It was a big event.

A teacher was on board. She would take off with the **astronauts**. She would teach lessons from space!

The launch seemed normal. Kids across the country watched eagerly. But then there was smoke. Flames burst out. The shuttle tore apart. The crew cabin crashed into the ocean. All seven people on board died.

## DID YOU KNOW?

In 1986, schools did not have the Internet. Children wanted to see the launch. NASA set up a special broadcast. Televisions in schools showed it.

# CHAPTER 2

# CHALLENGER

NASA had five space shuttles. **Rockets** launched them into space.

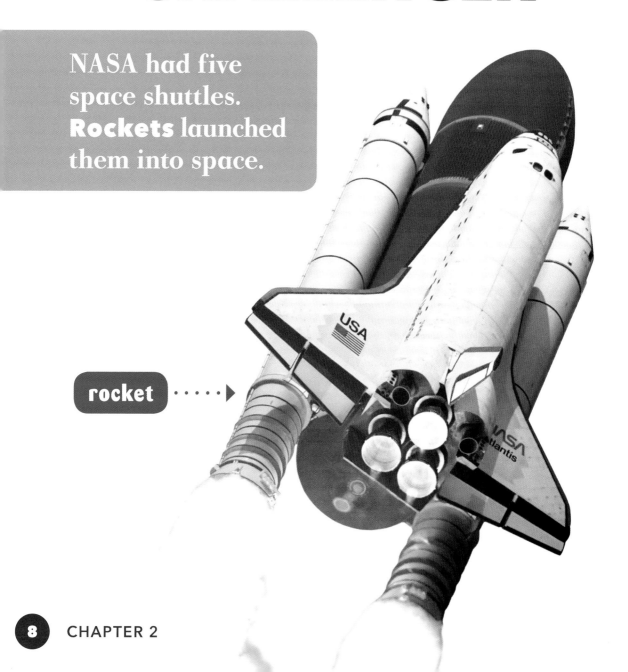

rocket ·····▶

They returned to
Earth like airplanes.

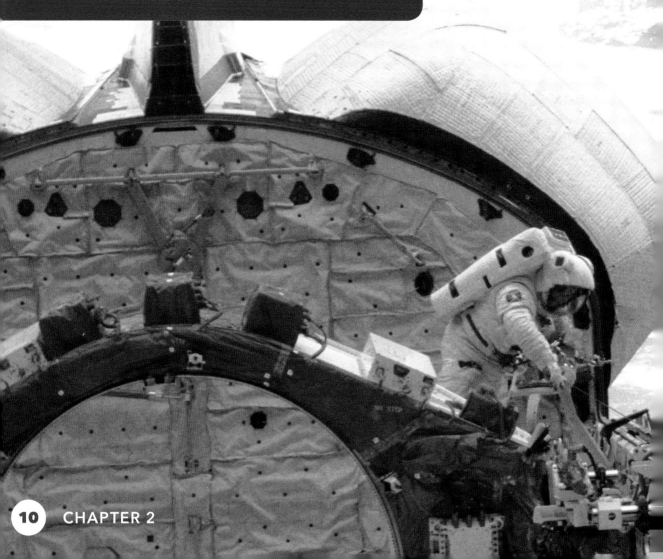

The shuttles had many jobs. They brought supplies to the **space station**. They made repairs. *Challenger* carried **satellites**. It was going to put them in space. The crew would also do tests.

# TAKE A LOOK!

How many parts does a shuttle have? More than 2.5 million! This diagram shows some of the main parts.

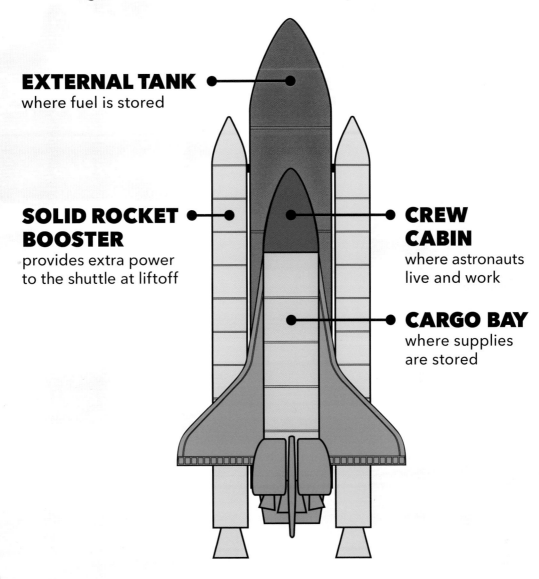

**EXTERNAL TANK**
where fuel is stored

**SOLID ROCKET BOOSTER**
provides extra power to the shuttle at liftoff

**CREW CABIN**
where astronauts live and work

**CARGO BAY**
where supplies are stored

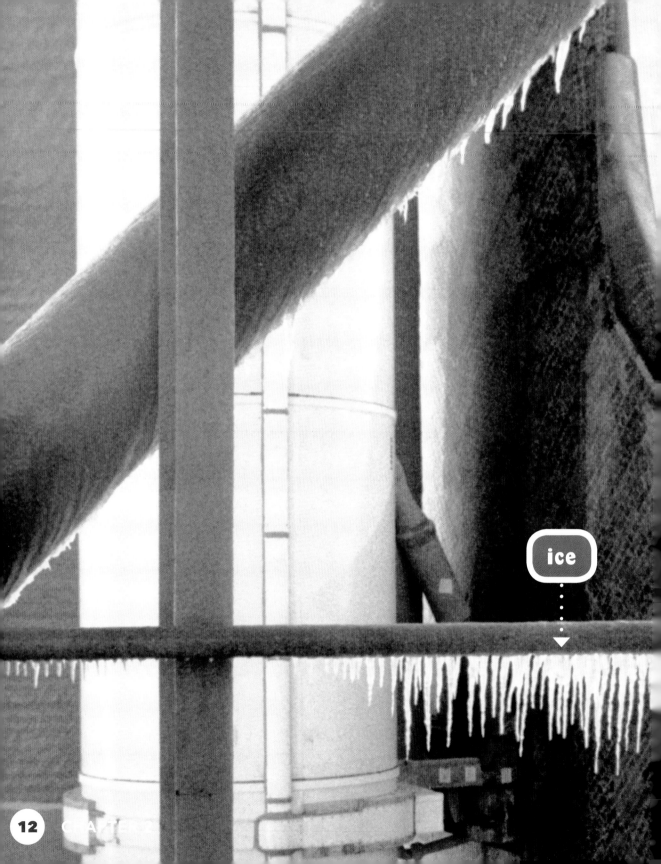

ice

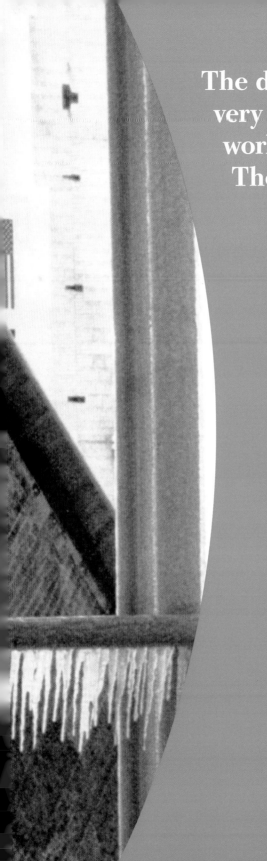

The day of the launch was very cold. That morning, NASA workers toured the launch site. They found ice.

The company that built the rocket boosters warned NASA. They said the weather was too cold for the rockets. But NASA decided to launch anyway.

At first things seemed to be fine. But that changed just 73 seconds later. The shuttle broke apart. Smoke and **debris** trailed down from the sky.

# CHAPTER 3

# WHAT WENT WRONG?

The disaster shocked the country. Everyone asked the same question. What went wrong? More than 120 people worked to find out. Who were they? Astronauts, **engineers**, and scientists.

They looked at **evidence**. They found pieces of the shuttle. They talked to people involved. They looked at past shuttle flights. Then they made a **report**. What did they learn?

shuttle piece

The report blamed the cold. It caused a seal in the rocket booster to become **brittle**. It cracked open. This sent out flames. The flames burned a hole in the shuttle's fuel tank. The fuel tank tore apart. It started on fire. The fire made the space shuttle break apart.

NASA had been warned. But they launched anyway. Bad decisions doomed the shuttle.

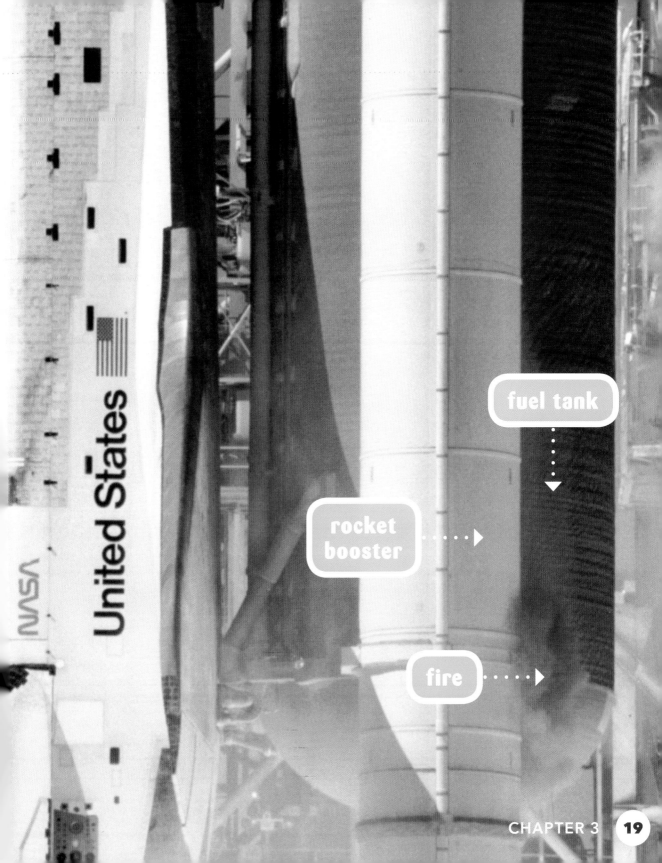

fuel tank

rocket booster

fire

The disaster had a huge impact. It changed the space program. It took two years before another shuttle was launched. The final shuttle flight was in 2011. NASA is working on other reusable space vehicles. NASA continues to reach for new heights.

### BALLOON SHUTTLE

**Did you know a balloon can work like a rocket engine? Try using a stream of fast-moving air to propel a paper shuttle forward.**

**What You Need:**

- cardboard
- piece of paper
- scissors
- tape
- 2 bendy straws
- balloon

1. **Fold the piece of paper into a paper airplane—any style.**

2. **Use the scissors to cut a rectangular shape approximately 6 inches (15 centimeters) by 4 inches (10 cm) out of cardboard.**

3. **Tape the paper airplane to the cardboard base [see illustration].**

4. **Now take the two straws and insert the non-bendy sides into the neck of the balloon. Seal with tape so no air can escape.**

5. **Tape the bendy end of the straws to the cardboard and the vertical lengths to the shuttle [see illustration].**

6. **Pick up your shuttle. Holding the neck of the balloon, blow into the bendy ends of the straws. When the balloon is filled, pinch your fingers together to hold the air inside. Then set down your shuttle on a flat, smooth surface and let it go!**

**astronauts:** People trained to command, pilot, or serve as a crew member of a spacecraft.

**brittle:** Easily broken, snapped, or cracked.

**debris:** The remains of something that has been broken down or destroyed.

**engineers:** People who use math and science to solve society's problems and create things that humans use.

**evidence:** Material that enables investigators to find the truth in a matter.

**NASA:** Abbreviation of National Aeronautics and Space Administration, the government agency that conducts space exploration.

**report:** A spoken or written account of something that one has observed, heard, done, or investigated.

**rockets:** Jet engines that get their thrust by burning fuel expelled as hot gas.

**satellites:** Spacecraft that are sent into orbit around Earth, the moon, or another heavenly body.

**space station:** An artificial satellite designed to stay in orbit permanently and to be occupied by humans for long periods.

# INDEX

# TO LEARN MORE

**Learning more is as easy as 1, 2, 3.**

1) Go to www.factsurfer.com

2) Enter "Challenger" into the search box.

3) Click the "Surf" button to see a list of websites.

With factsurfer, finding more information is just a click away.